Enlightenment

By Kit Kittle

Schiffer Publishing Ltd

4880 Lower Valley Road • Atglen, PA 19310

Dedication

For Laurette

Original Design by Claire Werner
Copyright © 2014 by Kit Kittle
Library of Congress Control Number: 2013958210

Type set in Democratica OT/Orpheus Pro

ISBN: 978-0-7643-4621-7
Printed in China

Schiffer Books are available at special discounts for bulk purchases for sales promotions or premiums. Special editions, including personalized covers, corporate imprints, and excerpts can be created in large quantities for special needs. For more information contact the publisher:

Published by Schiffer Publishing, Ltd.
4880 Lower Valley Road
Atglen, PA 19310
Phone: (610) 593-1777; Fax: (610) 593-2002
E-mail: Info@schifferbooks.com

For the largest selection of fine reference books on this and related subjects, please visit our website at www.schifferbooks.com.
We are always looking for people to write books on new and related subjects. If you have an idea for a book, please contact us at proposals@schifferbooks.com

This book may be purchased from the publisher.
Please try your bookstore first.
You may write for a free catalog.

contents

This is the face of the Buddha Dordenma that is outside Thimphu, Bhutan. The Buddha is sitting and the statue's height at the top of the head is over 130 feet. Inside the statue, there will be more than 100,000 smaller Buddha statues.

Introduction to Enlightenment

There is power in the image of the Buddha, a power I have felt for forty years. In 1972, when I was just sixteen, I went to the Buddhist Kingdom of Sikkim, a small country once bordered by Nepal, Bhutan, Tibet, and India, with my eighteen-year-old sister. Though we were there as teachers, we quickly found ourselves students of the lovely Sikkimese and their Indian friends. Both my sister and I wanted to learn more about Buddhism.

A week back in the states, I went to Woodberry Forest boarding school in Virginia for the start of my eleventh grade. Serendipitously, an alumnus named Joel McCleary came back to teach. Joel was a Harvard graduate who had just spent some time at the Buddhist Study Center in New Jersey run by Geshi Wangyal. He was twenty-three.

Every morning at six, Joel hosted about a half-dozen students in his unfurnished living room for an hour of sitting. It was much more difficult for us to be still than you might think. Most of us concentrated on breathing to quiet our minds. A few times someone sitting up straight would start snoring. One boy quit completely in the middle of a session, saying, "I can't do this." But mostly, we would sit there quietly for an hour.

At sixteen, this experience changed the way I see the world. Meditation led me to a state where I could see things more clearly because my mind was not chatting over what I was looking at. It is just that simple. In a photograph, everything is cleared away about a situation except the exact way it appears. It is much easier to see the way things look when your mind is quiet.

An interest in Buddhism lead me to study Sanskrit and philosophy at Benares Hindu University in India, where I spent my junior year living along the Ganges. Benares is a land of extremes, in both beauty and horror. It is a point of pilgrimage for devout Hindus whose bodies are always burning in funeral pyres along the Ganges. Benares also adjoins Sarnath, where Gautama Buddha walked to give his first lesson after his enlightenment twenty-five hundred years ago.

As a New York City kid, thanks to a best friend who set up a darkroom in his bathroom, I had been shooting photos, processing film, and making prints since fourth grade. In ninth grade, my parents gave me a Canon FTb single-lens reflex 35mm camera and an extremely sharp 50mm f1.2 lens. In India, it seemed that the only way to capture the otherness of Benares was to photograph it. I had my camera and twenty-five rolls of Kodachrome 25 film to last for eight months. Each frame had to count.

During my senior year at Kenyon College, my prints of Benares were hung up at the school bookstore and people I barely knew told me how unusual they were. Right after graduation, I took the slides to Air India in New York. They wanted to use them for marketing, but they had no money—only tickets. I had no money either.

I finally got a job working as a surveyor's assistant in the Brooks Range in the Alaskan arctic for a mining company. I spent my days walking along ridgelines with a reflector about two miles ahead of the surveyor and his theodolite. I worked more than three months before a day off but was thrilled by the wildness of the terrain. And I worked hourly.

One night, I sat on a steep ridge above our tents watching a herd of caribou backlit by the late night sun. Immersion in this natural beauty, right after the cultural beauty of Benares, led me to want to be a professional photographer. While walking, I now planned what I would do to make that happen.

Three days back from Alaska, I called Air India and traded the use of previously shot photos for three weeks in India on a press trip that had already started, along with additional first class tickets. The next day I was in India. This time it was all about photography.

I traveled the south of India and up into the Garwal Himalayas and visited my friends in Benares again. *Time* magazine and the Philadelphia Museum of Art bought the right to publish photos from that trip and assignments slowly started to appear.

This began thirty-five years of professionally shooting stills all over the world. My first book, *Roughnecks*, a photojournalist's look at oil field workers, came out twenty-nine years ago, published in 1985. Soon after, I married the book's designer and now we have two sons. One of my Caribbean clients, the island of Bonaire, asked me to direct a TV commercial for them and I shot my first 35mm motion picture film. Since then, I've directed TV commercials in China, Ireland, Venezuela, and Canada, and spots for financial companies and outdoor sports all over the U.S. But I've never stopped shooting photographs.

One day, my wife brought home this Buddha that she had found in a home shop. It is made of porcelain and weighs twenty-five pounds. I can just carry it, along with a small camera bag. I photographed this Buddha at my favorite places all around the woods and the river at home.

Then I started thinking about places that I'd have to drive to, places like the city and the beach. This Buddha comfortably fits in my convertible's passenger seat and is held steady by the seat belt. When we're cruising in the car, we look good.

It struck me that these photographs create a wonderful space for a few thoughts about what this Buddha means to our world. The Buddha connotes the importance of meditation and compassion in our daily lives. The story of his enlightenment is encouragement for all of us who struggle with our human predicament.

Most of the quotes assembled here have been among my favorites for decades. But this book is not at all "Buddhist". The Buddha can be seen less as a religious figure and more as a symbol of quiet and steadfast effort. Many people see the Buddha this secular way, Buddhists and non-Buddhists alike.

This Buddha is a great photography subject because its porcelain skin reflects the light around it. Its patina changes as the daylight goes by. In the outdoors, the Buddha seems to reflect the moods of nature. In other places, this Buddha can reflect the irony of a situation, like the peacefulness that can be found in commotion, or the loneliness that can be found in crowds..

May it also reflect some light for your path.

meditation

Don't just do something. Sit there!

Thich Nhat Hanh

Do not dwell in the past. Do not dream of the future.
Concentrate the mind on the present moment...

Buddhist teaching

To awaken, sit calmly, letting each breath clear your mind.

Buddhist teaching

If your mind is empty, it is always ready
for anything; it is open to everything.

Shunrya Suzuki

The quieter you become the
more you are able to hear.

Buddhist aphorism

Let the mind be empty, and not filled with the things of the mind.
Then there is only meditation, and not a meditator who is meditating.

Krishnamurti

Except your awareness, all is accidental.

Osho

The perfect man employs his mind as a mirror. It grasps nothing; it refuses nothing. It receives but doesn't keep.

Lao Tzu

Sitting quietly, doing nothing,
Spring comes, and the grass grows by itself.
Basho

Ask and it shall be given to you, seek and ye shall find, knock and it shall be opened unto you.

Matthew 7:7

Having no destination, I am never lost.

Ikkyu

As soon as you see something, you already start to intellectualize it. As soon as you intellectualize something, it is no longer what you saw.

Shunryu Suzuki

Truth is beautiful, without doubt; but so are lies.

Ralph Waldo Emerson

If you are unable to find the truth right where you are,
where else do you expect to find it?

Dōgen

The leafless cherry,
Old as a toothless man,
Blooms in flowers,
Mindful of its youth.

Basho

The winds that blow
Ask them which leaf of the tree
Will be the next to go.

Muso Soseki

What we are today comes from our
thoughts of yesterday, and our present
thoughts build our life of tomorrow.
Our life is the creation of our mind.

The Dhammapada

Sitting meditation is not, as is often supposed, a "spiritual exercise," a practice followed for some ulterior object.

Alan Watts

Things are in the saddle and
ride mankind.

Ralph Waldo Emerson

Do not speak unless it improves on silence.

Zen saying

Ego is constantly attempting to acquire and apply the teachings of spirituality for its own benefit.

Chogyam Trungpa

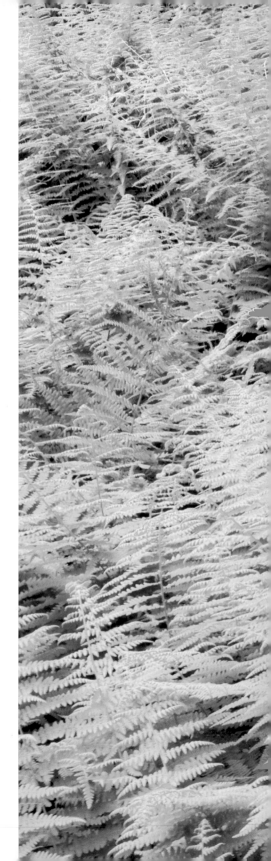

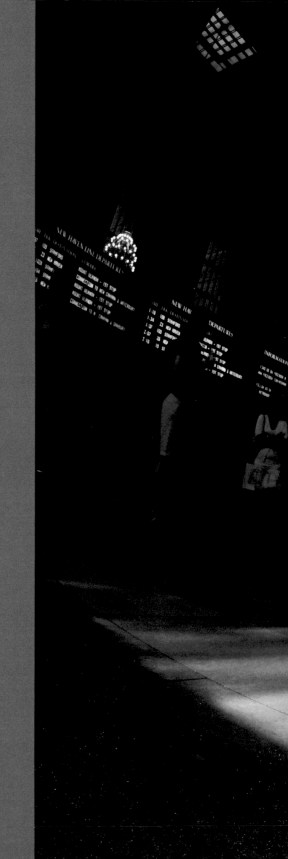

Happiness or sorrow–whatever befalls you,
walk on untouched, unattached.

The Dhammapada

Experience is not just what happens to you,
it is what you do with what happens to you.

Aldous Huxley

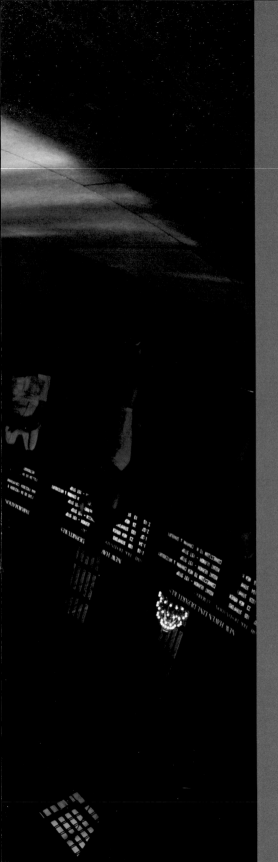

Happiness or sorrow—whatever befalls you,
walk on untouched, unattached.

The Dhammapada

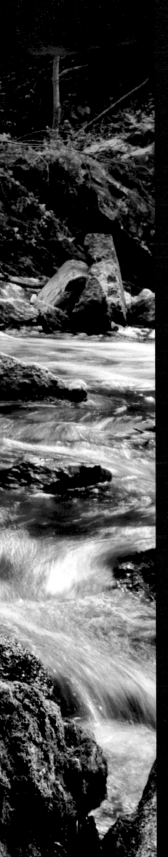

The whole secret of existence is to have no fear.
Never fear what will become of you.
Depend on no one.
Only the moment you reject all help are you freed.

Swami Vivekananda

Half an hour's meditation is essential, except when
you are very busy. Then a full hour is needed.

Saint Francis de Sales

The obstacle is the path.

Zen saying

Through examination we see the once-rigid ego dissolve into fiction, and the solidity of our world turns fluid.

Robert Thurman

If thou may not continually gather thyself together, do it some time at least once a day, morning or evening.

Thomas á Kempis

Don't think we can postpone meditation until we move or clean the garage.

Eknath Easwaran

The affairs of the world will go on forever. Do not delay the practice of meditation.

Milarepa

Compassion

The universe is change; our life is what our thoughts make it.

Marcus Aurelius

He experiences himself, his thoughts and feelings as something separated from the rest - a kind of optical delusion of his consciousness.

Albert Einstein

You have to start giving first and expect absolutely nothing.

H.H. The Dalai Lama

The level of our success is limited only by our imaginations and no act of kindness, however small, is ever wasted.

Aesop

My greatest wealth is the deep stillness in which I strive and grow and win what the world cannot take from me with fire or sword.

Johan Wolfgang Von Goethe

My religion is very simple. My religion is kindness.

H.H. The Dalai Lama

Kindness is ever the begetter of kindness.

Sophocles

If you want others to be happy,
practice compassion. If you want to be happy,
practice compassion.

H.H. The Dalai Lama

I'd like to offer you something, but in the Zen
school we don't have a single thing.

Ikkyu

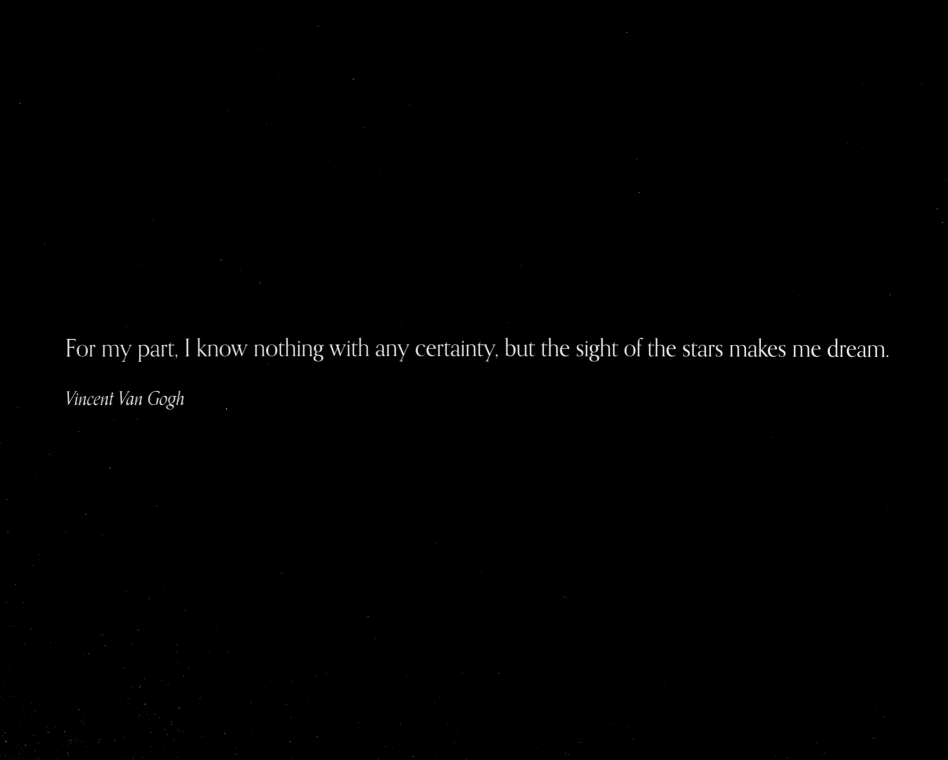

For my part, I know nothing with any certainty, but the sight of the stars makes me dream.

Vincent Van Gogh

Resolutely train yourself to attain peace.

The Buddha

We don't receive wisdom; we must discover it
for ourselves after a journey that no one can
take for us or spare us.

Marcel Proust

Truth is a pathless land.

Krishnamurti

We're fields of energy in an
infinite energy field.

E.E. Cummings

Not getting what you desire and getting what you desire can both be disappointing.

Buddhist aphorism

Take into account that great love and great achievements involve great risk.

H.H. The Dalai Lama

He begins to understand that self-observation is an instrument of self-change, a means of awakening.

George Gurdjieff

Slow down and the thing you are chasing will come around and catch you.

Zen saying

Encouragement

Winter is on my head, but eternal spring is in my heart.

Victor Hugo

When you reach the top,
keep climbing.

Zen saying

Thousands of
candles can be
lighted from a
single candle,
and the life of the
single candle will
not be shortened.
Happiness never
decreases by
being shared.

The Buddha

I seem to have been only like a boy playing on the seashore, and diverting myself in now and then finding a smoother pebble or prettier shell than ordinary, whilst the great ocean of truth lay all undiscovered before me.

Sir Isaac Newton

It no sooner comes than it is gone.

Each season is but an infinitesimal point.

It simply gives a tone and hue to my thought.

Henry David Thoreau

It has no duration.

The only Zen you can find on the tops of mountains
is the Zen you bring up there.

Robert M. Pirsig

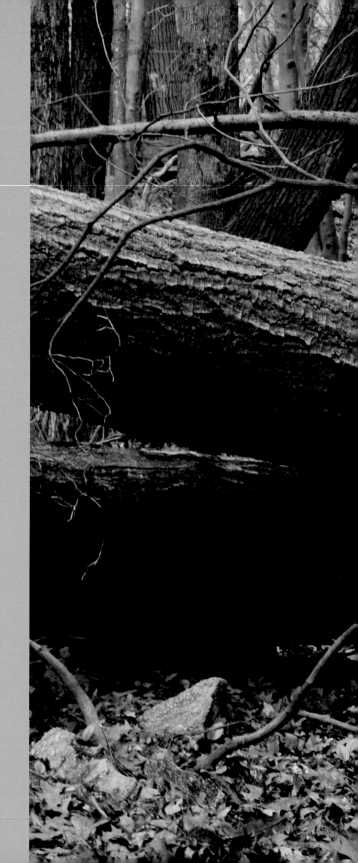

In the middle of the journey of our life, I came to myself within a dark wood where the straight way was lost.

Dante

Our life is an apprenticeship to the truth that around every circle another can be drawn; that there is no end in nature, but every end is a beginning, and under every deep a lower deep opens.

Ralph Waldo Emerson

What does a fish
know about the
water in which he
swims all his life?

Albert Einstein

Awake.
Be the witness of
your thoughts.

The Dhammapada

It's like clouds rising in the sky, suddenly there, gone without a trace. And it is like drawing a pattern on water; it is neither born nor passes away.

Ma-Tsu

Nothing in this world is more flexible and yielding than water. Yet when it attacks the firm and the strong, none can withstand it.

Lao Tzu

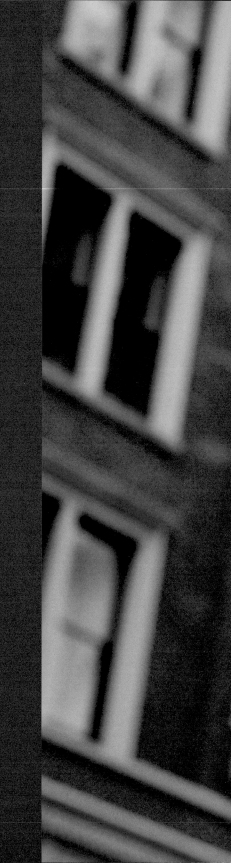

When walking just walk,
When sitting just sit,
Above all, don't wobble.

Yun Men

After enlightenment, the laundry.

Zen saying

Chance is always powerful.
Let your hook be always cast; in
the pool where you least expect
it, there will be a fish.

Ovid

At the end of all our exploring will be to arrive where we
started and know the place for the first time.

T.S. Eliot

Kit Kittle is a photographer and filmmaker
who travels the world on assignment.
He lives with his wife and two sons in
Greenwich, Connecticut.